T0114704

Taking Myself Apart and Putting People Together

(Finding Love, Happiness, and Yourself through Motivation)
By Dr. María Delua Sáenz and Sylvia Sáenz M.Ed.

Sylvia Sáenz M.Ed.

BALBOA.PRESS
A DIVISION OF HAY HOUSE

Balboa Press books may be ordered through booksellers or by contacting:

Balboa Press
A Division of Hay House
1663 Liberty Drive
Bloomington, IN 47403
www.balboapress.com
844-682-1282

Because of the dynamic nature of the Internet, any web addresses or
links contained in this book may have changed since publication and
may no longer be valid. The views expressed in this work are solely those
of the author and do not necessarily reflect the views of the publisher,
and the publisher hereby disclaims any responsibility for them.

The author of this book does not dispense medical advice or prescribe
the use of any technique as a form of treatment for physical, emotional,
or medical problems without the advice of a physician, either directly
or indirectly. The intent of the author is only to offer information
of a general nature to help you in your quest for emotional and
spiritual well-being. In the event you use any of the information in
this book for yourself, which is your constitutional right, the author
and the publisher assume no responsibility for your actions.

Any people depicted in stock imagery provided by Getty Images are
models, and such images are being used for illustrative purposes only.
Certain stock imagery © Getty Images.

Scripture quotations marked TLB are taken from *The Living Bible*
copyright © 1971. Used by permission of Tyndale House Publishers, Inc.,
Carol Stream, Illinois 60188. All rights reserved.

Print information available on the last page.

ISBN: 979-8-7652-4555-2 (sc)
ISBN: 979-8-7652-4554-5 (e)

Balboa Press rev. date: 09/18/2023

Preface

This book consists mostly of my mother's notes of the metaphysical classes she taught as well as her massage classes, and other classes she took. A few parts were channeled. Do your own research to verify facts.

My mom told me after she graduated to heaven "let go" in my dream. I thought it meant to release the past and memories of her but then I realized after a year when I did let go, I got closer to her Spirit and received a deeper connection.

This book is in honor of my mom who graduated to heaven and is still alive. Her greatest desire was to help as many people as possible. She wanted to write this book to let others know her story of pain, and how she got through her pain. By doing this, she felt it would inspire others in their journey of life to push through their pain and find the meaning of life by finding themselves and truly loving themselves.

The following is a letter from the year 1989 referring to the mentor of my family, Dr. Augustine Ramirez, how his impact had influenced me to make positive waves of change.

Those people who have entered our lives help to shape our lives like a ripple effect in a body of water have a significant role in our lives.

It is important to give the credit to those people who mattered in our lives and made a positive difference which goes on to other people who pass it on to others with God in charge orchestrating the events of our lives.

With the struggles that lead to victories in the end affects all of us.

Dear Dr. Kottman,

As for the reasons for my wanting an extension of my seven-year limit, the reasons are varied and complex. Perhaps the love for counseling began when I was in my mother's womb. For it was then that my mother met a great man who not only influenced my mother's life and mine but countless others who I have been able to touch through his true dedication in the field of helping others. For he was, still is a psychologist, and priest—Dr. Augustine Ramirez, an author and advocate of psychodrama and currently psycho-cybernetics. He got to study with Carl Rogers. Through him I was able to see the beauty of the individual and began my road to accepting others and myself as they are, and I am—what power.

I began my studies in counseling immediately after graduating in 1983. After the summer of 1983 I began teaching and continued to further my education. Among other courses, I took a personal growth class which helped, for in about a year, in 1984. I had an opportunity to really explore personal growth on a deeper level. I became involved with an alcoholic psychotic boyfriend which brought further insight about myself and put me further behind in my studies for I then to take a break from my classes to heal my cutting off from this relationship. Within a year, I attempted to continue my education by taking a class in Austin where I had to move to. Shortly afterwards, I got married and moved to Dallas. As I got my life in order with this new beginning, I hesitated starting school again for fear of another move for now I had to consider another person. After seeing that I would be settling in Dallas, I began to take classes after about 1 and ½ years of marriage. I realized my time limit was short, but I decided to go full speed ahead because finishing my degree meant being able to help children who could otherwise not be helped.

Working as a teacher, I became very sensitive to the needs of the children, but as I told the principal, playing both roles of counselor and teacher was exasperating.

I was having a little difficulty getting to attend college because of my GRE scores still I finally got permission to take classes. I can remember driving to college and crying, saying to myself: "why is it so hard for me to get the opportunity to help Hispanic children whom I teach?" Not even one counselor is available who can speak their language in the whole district.

Some of these children were from El Salvador. I will never forget a six-year-old child who shared with me "why do people kill one another?" His eyes watered about to cry, and I responded: "because they feel they cannot have what others have. They do not realize you can have things with love." I feel children whose dominant language is Spanish could benefit greatly with a bilingual counselor. I feel I can meet this need. In order to do so, I need a three-month extension from May of 1989 to August 1989, for the field experience course cannot be taken while I work and financially I need to work.

Thank you,

Sylvia Espiricueta

1   Taking Myself Apart and Putting People Together (Finding Love and Happiness and Yourself through Motivation) by Dr. María Delua Sáenz, and Sylvia Sáenz M.Ed.

Every person and every event counts. Living life to the fullest is the goal. What does that mean? Passion in life leads to success. Every belief and culture counts. Diversity makes life complete. My belief given to me by mom was that we choose our parents for a reason.

Even though my ego may not agree, my soul grows because of the environment I choose to grow up in, and the choices of myself and others that lead to life events.

And so it goes, I was born into a beautiful, wonderful family with its quirks of course.

In the summer of 1959, I met our family mentor, Dr. Father Augustin Ramirez, while in the womb of my mother.

My mother, young seventeen- year- old, naïve in Chicago, Illinois was dealing with opposition with new family in-laws. Dr. Ramirez notice by her walk that my mom was pregnant.

But before I begin my story, I feel compelled to explain her background life.

She began as 1st born baby in her family with her mother being only fourteen years old, a child herself. That was the time she decided to be born into my maternal grandparents' family.

My maternal grandparents were all about feelings, and really cared to know when they ask, "how are you?"

My mom gained her resourcefulness at the age of two when she was asked to go to the grocery store by her mother to get bread and milk. She learned to fend for herself at a young age.

She suffered abuse by teachers hitting her hands with rulers when she spoke Spanish. In her own words, "at the age of six years old in school I was asked what my name was. I would smile because I didn't know what they were saying. I was embarrassed. I didn't know English.

As a two and half year-old child I felt no one wanted me, because my mom didn't want to take care of me, so my grandmother did; so, I was going to take of myself and run away from home. So now when I don't like something I run."

She grew up defending her younger sisters. She would play "babeliche" (hopscotch), jacks and jump rope. She finished school in 8th grade and would work to earn money for her school clothes. She dreamed of having a lot of clothes like rich people do.

According to my mom, around the age of 10 when her father was looking for a new job, because they had moved from California to Texas so her mother could live near her mother, who was her maternal grandmother. Her mother, with tears in her eyes, told her that for Christmas, Santa Claus would not be able to find them. My mom responded: "I am positively sure Santa Claus will come. He knows everything." "I was visualizing at that age that he would come not knowing it was preparing me for the future of the goal setting group that I would offer people." "I proved to my mom that if you believe, it happens, because my father received a job and then an advanced cash payment." "Was I born with the gift or is it that when we come to earth we already know what we are supposed to do?"

My mom, Maria Gloria Delua, got married at the age of 16 years old to my father who wore a pink shirt and drove a pink chevy. My mother left her small town of Mercedes to join her husband in the big city of Chicago, Illinois. Feeling alone, she had no friends yet, even so my father would side with his mother in arguments that ensued between her and the in laws. At one instance, distraught, my mother decided to look for support and ended up walking to a Catholic Church to pray.

As fate would have it, she met an amazing man which was another major turning point in her life. The man she met was a Catholic priest and a psychologist. Dr. Father Augustin Ramirez, an inspiring mentor who made a huge difference.

Dr. Ramirez counseled her, and she began helping by counseling others in groups he organized. My mom learned about dealing with relationships. She developed her assertiveness which helped her self-worth.

3   Soon after she delivered, her first born, me, Sylvia. Living in poverty she protected her newborn from large hungry

rats which would enter the apartments, even though she was excessively clean herself as well as immaculately cleaning her own home. After awhile she went to work at a factory. Her second born, Zeferino II, my brother was born easily due to constant squatting she had to do in the factory.

Leaving her factory job, she went to work as a nurse aide, and later as a teacher aide. As a teacher aide, she was much appreciated by the principal, Ms. Carson, who depended on her people skills to persuade gang members to cooperate and hand over guns.

Mom saw beauty in everything from the yellow bird at her rehab to patterns and colors on ceiling at the ICU and to the beauty of all people's hearts.

She also put her social skills talent into her nurse aide job, where she was extremely dedicated to give her all, passionately with all her love and compassion.

Part of self-love involves not being so hard on oneself with self-judgment, and self-criticism. Being able to laugh at oneself to grow and learn.

On the frigid mornings in Chicago, my mom walked with my brother and I telling us stories to get our minds off the cold. We looked forward to walking to school thoroughly enjoying her vivid imagination.

Time went by and my sister, who I had prayed for her to be born, Sonia was born when I was eight years old. She slept in the pantry because it was only a three-bedroom home. Eventually she slept in my bedroom, until I became an adult, and we bought a four-bedroom home.

By the time I was in fourth grade, my mom made sure I was tested which helped to place me in a high intelligence creative classroom where I fell in love with education even more because I was allowed to do my original work of projects and essays like ghost stories.

Like night and day, since 3rd grade was a nightmare because our teacher would lock up children in closet who misbehaved.

At the end of my 4th grade my mom had a critical decision to make. She said no to getting scholarship to obtain a nursing degree. She said yes to moving to the Rio Grande Valley in order to keep her children safe from crime and also to realize my father's dream of owning his own transmission shop.

Life is full of critical turning points based on our decisions. So, the family left to start a new beginning back at a small hometown in McAllen, Texas. I was ten years old. My brother was eight years old, and my sister was only two years old.

Starting all over was exciting but scary. Our family was doing their best to improve their economic situation.

Shortly after getting to the Rio Grande Valley, my mother suffered a great loss of her fourth child, a son, when she miscarried. She felt totally lost again, with an unbearing deep hole hurt. A void that couldn't be quenched with anything but God's plan.

So, her adventure began from studying the Rosicrucian's', Silva Mind Control, and every single religion she could find to explain the reason for her loss. She was learning about self-love, God's miraculous presence so she could become complete.

Funny how a hole in your heart leads to planting a seed in that hole that grows into your new purpose which you were meant to do all along.

In South Texas, like in many places, metaphysical studies were rare to find especially during the 1970's. After mom finished her Doctorate degree in Metaphysics, which she humbly kept a secret, she began her group Love and Happiness through Motivation in 1978. Her goal was to empower women to manifest their dreams. And boy did she!

The group consisted of goal setting, meditation, visualization, seeing chakras, and so much more.

This metaphysical group granted these students desires to be materialized. My mom's lost, hurt with a hole, planted a seed with her quest to master spirituality studies that led her to help other souls grow.

Her metaphysical group named Love and Happiness through Motivation lasted about 12 years.

Let's Enter My Mom's Classroom

Love and Happiness through Motivation by Divine Light based on King Tut teaching

Her group was to teach others to find happiness and themselves through motivation by loving themselves and finding their importance in this world.

By changing attitudes from negative to positive and through that God gives us power.

Life Is like a balancing act. She said to plant seeds but when appropriate to let go. I thought letting go was so I wouldn't remember her anymore but it was to become more spiritual so I could feel her more in a different capacity.

All meetings started and ended with a prayer from different members of the group. Everyone would take a turn changing weekly.

My mother's groups lessons came from Silva Mind Control, Rosicrucian, Confederación Espirita Mexicana, countless more organizations. My mother, Maria Gloria Delua Saenz, counselor, earned a Ph. D. in metaphysics.

Sylvia Sáenz M.Ed.

She was a registered massage therapist, Texas license #3900. My mom said, "I hope my story helps someone out there who feels they are too old, or too sick to achieve." "You too can do anything you want to if you think you can you can." She earned her Ph.D. in Theology. She was a nurse aide for five years, a factory worker punch press for one year, saleslady at Montgomery Ward for 20 years, massage therapist for ten years, teacher aide for two years, and a Metaphysical Spiritual Leader for twelve years. She had great social skills and was offered a college scholarship in nursing.

Mom's message:

"Let go of people telling you what to do. I am a child of God. Put yourself in the white light so you don't you get the sickness of other people. Dreams help relate to what happens in my life. What do your dreams mean? You can learn through practice. Keep a dream log. When you are awakened write it down."

"Love is letting go of fear, Gerald G. Jamplsky. Hypnotism is done by letting go of each part of your body. To let yourself know, look in the mirror and say, 'I am love.'"

Eliminate completely	Make these words part of your vocabulary
I can't	I can
Doubt	I expect the best
I'm afraid	I am confident

Can verses Can't

Cancel Negative

Others are our Mirror-Others negative or positive is our negative or positive

"Slow me down dear Lord and inspire me to send my roots deep into the soul of the lives enduring values that I may grow toward the stars of my greater destiny."

Born to Win James Gerward.

Hypnosis Alpha same suggestion is planted in the subconscious mind. You can be hypnotized by radio, TV, newspapers, and magazines.

1. Beta – we think more of the body, doing, and thinking. We use mind, body, and spirit.
2. Alpha-we have answer programming.
3. Theta-4 to 7 brain waves per second.
4. Delta-deep trance sleep.

Ask yourself: what will be on my tomb stone?

Do not be a slave to your anger.

We change every day. If we can't keep something, it's because we need to learn something from that, so it won't happen again." I can do all things through God." Nothing is more spiritual than a clean body, mind, and soul. "The day we stop wanting we die. What God wants it will be."

The brain's function has two hemispheres. The left hemisphere controls logic and the right hemisphere controls creativity.

Left Hemisphere

Logical

Language

Skills

Speech/Words

Reading

Writing

Dates/Names

Mathematics

Controls the right side of the body

Right Hemisphere

Creativity

Intuition

Imagination

Emotions/Feelings

Controls left side of the body

"We have electrical energy to do anything. We are energy like acupuncture therapy, massage, the laying of hands, and meditation. Food and everything that grows has energy."

"Energy light entering and being transmitted back to visual cortex is manipulated to make objects appear."

Mom spoke about goal setting and finding your inner guide.

She taught about colors:

> Yellow- expanding wisdom
>
> Dark Blue- powerful
>
> Dark Brown- depressing
>
> White- gives freedom
>
> Green- healing growth
>
> Red- heart condition/passion
>
> Pale Blue and White- honesty, morality in home
>
> Pale Green- for hyperactive child

Mom's messages:

"If you do a lot of thinking you don't put your ideas into action."

"If you ask angels for help, they help you." "You are unique, the only one in the universe like you." "Hunches and intuition come from angels." "A man broke a glass. Why does it bother you so much? What's you're feeling?" "More than anything accept "Lesson: Putting an end to self-punishment." "Did you change negative to positive? Did you write the goal and do the picture?

Sylvia Sáenz M.Ed.

"Write: Did I gain anything when I did this? If so, what?"

"Write: Did I lose anything when I did this? If so, what?"

"Write: Could I have handled the situation another way? If so, in what way?"

"How did it make you feel? How might it make others feel?"

"Stand before a mirror and look at yourself, in your eyes, use positive words."

"Talk to your body. Explain that you are willing to do anything that is needed to help it recover. Your body will cure itself."

Exercise: "I love myself therefore I'm doing the best I can."

"I approve of myself exactly as I am." "I am willing to release all resistance." "I forgive you for not being the way I wanted you to be." "I forgive you and set you free."

"The human mind can and does generate force fields." "A field of energy can appear from a human, animal or plant."

"But everyone wants to talk about themselves, and no one wants to hear."

"I am willing to change and to grow. I now create a safe new future (chronic diseases)."

"It is my birthright to live fully and freely. I love life. I love me. (Emphysema)"

"I see with love and joy. I now create a life I love to look at. (eyes)"

"I rejoice in my femaleness. I love being a woman. I love my body. (Female problems)"

"I love and approve of myself. I see myself and what I do with the eyes of love. I am safe. (headaches)"

"I release all that is unlike love. There is time and space for everything I want to do. (hemorrhoids)"

"My thinking is peaceful calm, centered. (inflammation)"

"My good comes from everywhere and everyone. All is well in my world."

To sell: "All my possessions are sold easily and quickly."

"The move is very simple to do."

"Everything is working in Divine right order. All is well."

"I love myself therefore _____."

"I have a beautiful new car and it comes to me easily."

"I have a beautiful new house and it comes to me easily."

"Love who you are and what you do."

"Laugh at yourself and at life."

"Be thankful for all the good in your life_____. It will bring more good."

"List all the things you are willing to let go of."

Work

"I love myself therefore I work at a job I truly enjoy doing, one that uses my creative talents and abilities, with people I love and love me, as well as earning a good income."

"I am totally receptive to a wonderful new position, one that uses all of my talents and abilities, allowing me to express creatively in a way that is fulfilling to me."

"I love and approve of myself. I am at peace. I am calm. All is well.'

Exercise: Negative messages:

Inner child feels unsafe. He/She needs comfort. If afraid or angry say: "I am no longer helpless. I can do this."

"I am worthy of the very best in life. I now lovingly allow myself to accept it."

Exercise

In a relaxed comfortable position say: "I am willing to let go. I release all tension. I release all fear. I release all anger. I release all guilt. I release all sadness. I let go of all old limitations. I am at peace with myself."

"Life is for me." "I am at peace with the process of life. I am safe."

Release anger by beating a pillow, playing tennis, running, etc.

Release negative feelings by saying "I deserve to have everything I have and more. I accept it now! I'm doing the best I can."

"This is one of the best days of your life. Everything is working out for your highest good. Whatever you need to know is revealed to you. Whatever you need comes to you. All is well."

"I love and approve of myself. I create my own joy. I choose to be a winner in life. (colitis)"

"This child responds only to love and to loving thoughts. All is peaceful. (colic)"

"I relax and allow my mind to be peaceful. (cramps)"

"I relax and let life flow through me with ease. (Gas pains)"

"I love you _ (your name) _. In the infinity of life where I am all is perfect, whole, and complete."

"My unique creative talents and abilities flow through me and are expressed in deeply satisfying ways."

"There are people out there who are always looking for my services. I am always in demand and can pick and choose."

"I earn good money doing what satisfies me. My work is a joy and a pleasure. All is well in my world."

"Divine Intelligence gives me all the ideas I can use. Everything I touch is a success. There is plenty for everyone including me. There are plenty of customers seeking my service."

"I establish a new awareness of success. I win into the winning circle. I am a magnet for Divine prosperity. I am beyond my fondest dreams. Golden opportunities are everywhere for me. I bless my front door knowing that only good comes into my home. I expect my life to be good and joyous and it is."

"I am willing to release the pattern in my consciousness that has created this condition! I release that pattern in me that created this. I am at peace. I am worthwhile."

"I now discover how wonderful I am. I choose to love and enjoy myself."

"I love and accept myself at every age. Each moment in my life is perfect."

"The world is safe and friendly. I am safe. I am at peace with life."

"I easily and comfortably release that which I no longer need in my life."

"I love and approve of myself. I trust the process of life. I am safe."

"It is safe now for me to take charge of my own life. I choose to be free."

"I comfortably and easily release the old and welcome the new in my life."

Sylvia Sáenz M.Ed.

"In my world I am my own authority for I am the only one who thinks in my mind."

"Letting go is easy. I freely and easily release the old and joyously welcome the new. I am loving the operator of my mind."

"It is easy for me to reprogram the computer of my mind. All of life is change and my mind is ever new."

"I am free to be me. I allow others the freedom to be who they are. It is safe for all of us to grow up."

"It is my birthright to live life fully and freely. I am worth loving. I now choose to live life fully."

"I declare peace and harmony with me and around me. All is well."

"I relax and allow my mind to be peaceful."

"I am peaceful with all my emotions. I love and approve of myself."

"I relax and let life flow through me with ease."

"I am a decisive person. I follow through and support myself with love."

"Ego equals past and future that is not real. What you learn is that you are a free soul."

"And you can do what you want to because no one is better than the other."

"I can't let others hurt me because I can't hurt others or myself."

"When anger comes, feel your feeling. The unconscious mind feels the anger, hate, and hurt."

"Do you believe in God? Many times, you will say there is no God. Why? God is good. God is love, power, and energy."

"It starts from childhood. Self-esteem is just an idea we have about ourselves on our worth and power. Power is the ability to take care of ourselves in everyday life."

"Especially when the going gets rough, self-esteem is a picture we have in our mind about ourselves."

"In early childhood we begin listening to the opinions and tone of everyone important to us like our parents, teachers, family, and friends. We listened and watched to see how they treated us. We take what they say and do judge ourselves."

"We hide our feelings inside ourselves, because at a young age we can not think for ourselves nor know that we are unique because God only made one of us. We are valuable and loveable. Then for the rest of our lives our answer became our true story."

"We change ourselves, our ideas, feelings, opinions, and pictures of ourselves. What we say and do about ourselves can change because God is in us."

"We behave as we value ourselves. We take the easy way out like doing what is familiar or comfortable. Then later we feel bad for a long time. After that we learn to speak up for what we need and refuse abuse from anyone even those who are important to us."

"Help us change our minds about ourselves with new self-idea seeds. Take deep root with your ideas. Treat others like yourself because they are like us, even if they're weird and unexplainable."

Love

"How many kinds of love are there? There is the love of the Devine, love of God. God is love and love is God. God without limits loves all people. God says love your enemies. Do good to them and pray for them."

"Human love is based in personality and selfish lawless fickle. (The Living Bible, The Way) Genesis 2:18 God said 'It is not good for man should be alone. I will make a companion for him, a helper suited to his needs.'"

"So, we go to the love of man and woman. When two people discover each other, a new life begins that is radiant and wonderful. Even poets you know in your heart, God being one of them with mansions he wants for your joy."

"Greek legend- two souls stand together like two great trees for sunshine and storm. Love enters not through a door but by heart. Love comes to the plain, just as to pretty, to the rich and poor. (The Living Bible, The Way) 1 John 4:7 "Beloved let us love one another for love is of God."

"So, then children come. They give love and want care. We live for them, and they live for us. Sometimes we forget that they belong to themselves. God makes each of us, one of a kind, and we as parent, teach our children, the best we know. We let them know they are miracles and unique. They show us love and we learn from them as much as they learn from us." 17

"Our children have mansions on earth, so they go their way. So, you grow apart. No need to hate the other. No need to fight."

"How do I fine love? The more people you love the more radiant you will become. Love all men and women. Others will turn to you as flowers turn to the sun."

"God has not given me the element of fear, but the power of love and a sound mind. I am not afraid. I have power in Jesus Christ."

"Divine Love is forgiving yourself."

"Put the white light of God to protect me from all harm and negativity. I am safe."

"I let go of anger and put it in God's hands. I can do all things through God."

"You are here to find the key to love yourself. Denial of love is a refusal to forgive."

"Don't look for someone else to love you and forgive you. You must do it first to be happy. Love yourself. Forgive yourself."

"I am glad to talk to you. I hope in what I say today I will help you in your growth. We all have our own reality because we choose what we want to be."

"Whenever you need hope I give you more than living for today and tomorrow because there is more to life. We have here to choose reality. Yes, you want a house, car, job, to marry, to have fun, to fly but the beginning comes from loving yourself and forgiving yourself. You judge yourself and feel not good enough. We have a saying everything happens for the best but you can make the best for yourself today."

Hypnosis

"Hypnosis helps a lot in self growth for people to do better in their lives."

"You can start by sitting in a comfortable chair. Settle down. Adjust your breathing to a slow relaxed manner."

"As you exhale imagine that you are releasing tensions of the day. As you inhale breathe in and out tell yourself with open eyes what you would like to do. Descending numbers you become more and more relaxed. Tell your subconscious mind, accept, and act upon the suggestions you give it. Affirm it.

Aura

"All things are possible to him who believes." (The Living Bible, The Way) Mark 9:23

(The Living Bible, The Way) Hebrews 11:3 "all things were made at God's command and that they were all made from things that can't be seen."

"It is difficult for you to understand why I God lives in us, we have trouble and wrong thoughts. God makes men in his image, so He loves us and give us a lot of energy that we are learning about."

23

"Currents of energy magnetic colored, the etheric body-outer body and inner body comes from the skin forming an electromagnetic field around the physical body."

"Sensitive when light falls upon the body. Different types of light aura say a story of each person's health and wounds. Plants have an aura that's why after working in the yard, you feel good. Go sit by a tree."

(The Living Bible, The Way) 1 Corinthians 6:19: "Haven't you learned that your body is the home of the Holy Spirit God gave you, and that he lives within you."

(The Living Bible, The Way) John 15:16: "You didn't choose me! I chose you! I appointed you to go and produce lovely fruit always, so that no matter what you ask for from the Father, using my name, he will give it to you."

"Have you opened your mind to receive the word which means to accept? To receive we must accept mentally first. As a child of God, you have no right to limit yourself with false ideas."

Charles Fillmore has declared in his book: "we cannot be very happy if we are poor, and nobody needs to be poor. It is a sin."

As the Bible promises all things are yours. Money is spiritual, and part of our spiritual heritage. "Gold" appears more than four hundred times in the Bible.

When Jesus said how hard it will be for those who trust in riches to enter the kingdom. He knows that the rich man was possessed by his possessions rather than controlling them.

Desire is God trying to give you greater good. Open your mind to receive it. Writing it down so that you manifest with choice words. You are so wrapped up in problems of the past and the present that you don't make the time to plan for better things. Are you hostile or envious of people around you who succeed? Do you criticize them? How do you feel? Unkind remarks stop blessings.

Sometimes we are tested. Sometimes the good we desire in life seems to come to people around first. If we can give praise and give thanks for another blessing rather than to be envious, jealous, and critical then we can be assured that those same blessings or even greater ones will come to us.

22 Always when making desires write at the bottom: "This or something better Father." "Let your unlimited good will be done."

"I prefer to give to where it helps and spiritually inspire many people. When you do not give you do not receive."

To clean your mind, clear your house closets, drawers, filing cabinets, desks, and car garage. Forgive others and decree Jesus Christ in the situation you have been unable to resolve.

Create your prosperity mentally first and then in writing.

End of Love and Happiness through Motivation Group

My mom's legacy continues with me. She wanted the world to know how special each of us are. It was important for the world to know it starts with self-love and then helping others.

One of her favorite sayings was "with God all things are possible."

The other of her many sayings was "cry for 5 minutes then move on." What she meant was not to stay stuck in self-pity but to be aware of feelings then go to joy, love, and fun.

One of her students had a lot of requirements to make her dreams a reality. It did take her a little longer, but her dreams did become a reality. So, all her students did achieve their goals! That achievement level of without limits was instilled into her children. She also encouraged (animaba) her husband who helped us from poverty to upper middle class! She worked, clipped coupons, and looked for bargains. Together they sticked to a strict budget. Amazing!

My mom wanted people to believe in their power. She asked me to write a song about believing. I wrote two songs about believing. "Belief makes it possible," she said. She came from humble beginnings both in wealth but also in limited emotional support into a new city from a small town.

She met up with Dr. Father Augustin Ramirez, a mentor who changed our lives for the better.

Lessons that I Learned from my Mom

She would say you have five minutes to cry to teach me to move forward from sadness after it had served its purpose.

Don't praise yourself. Let others do it! (The Living Bible, The Way) Proverbs 27:2

When things break put water on it and then throw away to safeguard against negativity. You avoided evil coming to you.

"You don't have to breathe if you don't want to," meaning you always have a choice.

Can't cry over spilled milk. What you lost another needed it.

Everyone is your mirror. What you see in others is in you.

Say "Cancel! Cancel! Cancel!" to get rid of negative thoughts. She learned this from Silva Mind Control.

No hay mal que por bien no venga. There's no bad that doesn't bring good.

From Success Motivation Institute Wheel of Life for 6 major areas: spiritual, family, mental, physical, financial, and social.

Choice of words is important. My mother's student reminded me to change crazy to exciting and after I did my life became more exciting. Say: "how can it get better than this?" Also say "That's wonderful. I'm next."

She taught me "the magic was already in you."

Mom's song:

I want to be tree, free, free!

Like the birds up in the tree, tree, tree!

Just together you and me, me, me!

Sylvia Sáenz M.Ed.

I also learned from my mom (The Living Bible, The Way Romans 8:31) "If God is with us who can be against us!"

Mom's song:

God's Light

I am whole! I am free! I have that special light in me!

Jesus sends from above giving me peace and love.

(Forever, whenever in God light!)

I am perfect. I am perfect. I am free!

Lessons from my mom continue

Everyone is your mirror and reflects what's going on in you.

Make positive affirmations to the mirror to reach your soul.

Set your goals in writing including the date to be achieved. Am I willing to accept responsibility that goes with the fulfillment of those desires? What am I going to give up making room for my desires? After making a list, bless then release to the Father.

Charles Fillmore discovered that there is power in the name of Jesus Christ. Jesus Christ now manifests the perfect typist to produce this quickly.

By pure white light of the Christ into which nothing negative could penetrate and out which only good can come. Jesus

Christ taking control of his souls, our marriage, our health, and guiding every step of the way in a tranquil miracle.

The Lord's Prayer is powerful because it tunes you into the same miracle consciousness that Jesus had for manifesting prosperity like when he multiplied the loaves of bread and fish to feed thousands. Repeating the Lord's Prayer is a great success formula for invoking healings.

Peace of mind, vitality, right action in one's affairs, prosperity, and guidance as well as great power for breaking up and dissolving difficult conditions quickly. As you use it daily, great prayer may even shock you into greater good than you have ever known.

Sayings

"Love fills me and heals me as I open to connect with people that God has placed in my life."

"Today I seek spiritual understanding beyond everything else. I choose peace, love, and joy as my goals."

"The spiritual understanding of the individual is the only understanding required for peace." Shirley McLane

"Thoughts and words create our future experience." Louise Hay

"We will not regret the past nor wish to shut the door on it." The Big Book Alcoholics Anonymous

"Today I can look back with love in my heart, knowing that every moment, every experience of my life has been necessary, valuable, and significant."

"Life is what happens to us while we are making other plans." Thomas La Mance

"Nobody can help more than what you help yourself. It is better to have to do a job than to holler for help. Do it yourself and you have a better chance. The important thing is to do your best. Remember always the game is not about winning or losing but how you play the game. Play the game with rules. You will win even if you lose. In life we struggle. Don't ever cheat yourself by playing it safe. Nobody was ever greater than the difficulties he overcame. Small difficulties make people small while big difficulties make people big.

School is always important in training the mind as sports is important in the training the body. In one way, however, sports are better than books or exams. It is hard to cheat at sports. Struggle is your friend. Without it, you can go no place. Only struggle toughens your muscles and your mind.

How can you see the good if you have only good? There has to be bad to see the good.

To live on a different level, you would take a different step of life. Pain comes when you must grow. If you do bad, it will come back to you. There is always change that can be made. God gives you a choice to do what you want

Pan American University November 14, 1984

The person who follows the crowd and doesn't choose his or her identity, living passionately can not be said to really exist.

After my mom instructed her classes for self-growth, she became a registered therapist.

Most people who believe in God believe in life hereafter.

1. If you're looking at yourself what is the most important thing that you can say about who you are? (I did this. I am feeling that.)

2. Do you have a self? And if so, how can you say you have it?

28 Yes, there is a self or a soul. Buddha does not believe in a soul, but in energy reborn. Answer for yourself: who went to the store or to the house, and so on?

What are you? Everyone changes every seven years.

The purpose of being on earth is to learn how to live. Learning how to live is an art. Man is something. He is not a "nothing."

I am a beautiful child of an undying God, inheriting the same undying principles.

Infancy and during those tender years we behave as a child. We think as a child. The voice, the form, the look in your eyes change.

We take from our parents' and teachers' qualities that became ours.

We have memories of sadness and happiness. If we grow childish, we never put aside childhood.

In youthful adolescence we dance and fly high mentally. We break rules of games and play. We rebel, reform and mature. We take with us the pattern of youthful memories including some scars, some bad seeds, some blossoms, and a measure of knowledge about we experienced.

When you have to say who you are then you know who you are.

I feel people can change to have a different way of thinking.

Human body and soul go together. I open my mind self.

We don't see the change because it so small but there is a change every three minutes.

How do you look in the world?

The Powerhouse ———-Inner True Self———-Feeling.

Mask———-outer false self, things we have learn.

We see one thing and think another.

The soul goes on living. You need the body to know who is (name).

The soul or spirit would make the person. What you act out will come to be.

No one will remember you one hundred years from now. The soul is a feeling. The feeling you have on earth. What you take with you is the feeling.

We are what we believe. As a man thinks in his heart he is. (The Living Bible, The Way, Proverbs 23:7)

Reincarnation/ Self-improvement

If your life isn't the way you consciously want it to be, there is a subconscious programming that must be overcome. Your conscious and subconscious are in conflict as a result of past programming in this life or in a previous lifetime.

If God punishes, he certainly wouldn't punish without a reason. Yet we obviously punish ourselves when we need to atone for past misdeeds even if we are mistaken. Even if we didn't do anything wrong although we think we did.

If we did not have problems, you would have to invent some to give yourself the opportunity to grow and learn to make your life. The bigger the problem, the bigger the opportunity. The problem usually stays with us just as long as we need it to achieve an understanding for ourselves. Once we understand we can let go of the effect.

Sylvia Sáenz M.Ed.

A master accepts others as they are without attempting to change them to be what he wants them to be.

In Hindu's view spirit no more depends on the body it inhabits. We outgrow a suit or find our house too cramped, so we exchange for a roomier one that offers our bodies more free play.

We have all seen the caterpillar turn into a butterfly, but do you know it undergoes three or four sheddings of skin.

Man is not a victim of cyclic karmic law, but man has the power to change his course and use it to reach the height of perfection. To stand up to what you discover often requires courage.

Technique for re-organizing/starting a new life

What is your purpose in living for the future?

What do you want of life?

Is your goal money or personal achievement?

Analyze your past mistakes.

Questions

What mistakes did I make?

What should I avoid in the future?

Do I have a desire to achieve greatness?

Do I let myself be influenced negatively?

Whose fault, is it?

What are your surroundings?

Is there harmony for myself and members of my family?

Everything that has happened to you even your failures, your disappointments, your heartaches, and your sufferings have been for a purpose. Nothing in the cosmic scheme is ever without purpose.

It is your prerogative to change the thoughts you have entertained and to reprogram your mind with new concepts. Don't live for the time when things will change for you. Instead change things for yourself by using the today you have today. Live right now by living right now! Use each tick of the clock to make a new beginning for yourself. It is not the experience of sleep or death that changes a person. It is the experience of life.

1) Breaking the attitude of unhappiness.
2) Don't frown. Smile.
3) Change words of complaint to words of optimism.
4) More self-assured than when she began. Started more positive.

Each tick of the clock is a new beginning for me. Nothing from past can take precedence over my present. I program my mind now with new thoughts of success, and a new cycle of experience begins.

Sylvia Sáenz M.Ed.

San Antonio, Dr. Robert Chaney Seminar, July 12, 1985

If someone is angry try to breath the same as them. Anger will go away. So, breathe with the other person so you can better relate to each other.

Picture your mind, white light, getting white on your face, your higher self.

Breathing Exercise for ESP

1) You are in a forest, waterfall, pool, having a wonderful time. There are people having fun.
2) You are in the sea, and you hear the water. You feel the sand. You're alone.

Use your mind to do anything you want to do. Use your mind and you'll get what you want. God said ask and you shall get it. Little successes give big success.

There are Three kinds of Meditation

Contemplative—my mind wanders you might say but you are in meditation.

Responsive—receive a thought from someone.

Casual candlelight —to send out something, healing or white light.

Say thank you to your body after it gives you what you want.

Visit the person before in your mind and the next day should be better.

We all have a mission to do on earth. Hell is a state of mind. We have done wrong and good. We look at the Akashic Records. When we go back in time, when we die, some people hurry back. Others will stay. We cannot come back if we are not ready. Pets have souls too. God keeps records of all your past lives.

If you lose money don't worry, go looking for it. Just sit down and ask for the record. You learn a lesson.

July 14, 1985, 10:00 –Take care of your body. It is your job to do it. They say we are going to use the mind to take care of your body. There will come a time when you don't have to take care of it for it will be filled with another person's feeling. There is power in healing everything on earth like herbs. See yourself getting well and you will be healthy. Like when you smile and walk by a tree, the white light of God shines. Your hands, eyes, feet move when you ask them to with your mind. So, you can see how the mind works. Your attitude is what gets you up or does not. What do you want out of life? What do you live for?

Our family mentor was Dr. Father Augustine Ramirez, Ph.D. in Psychology from Catholic University, Washington D.C. in 1955. He had three publications including Mind Modern Man. He wrote psychodrama books. He studied psychodrama, including Gestalt Therapy. He knew seven languages.

Dr. Augustine Ramirez said if a child is used by his parents, he can become a psychopath. If a child is shown love, he will be self-confident. If a child's love is unrecognized, then the child will grow up to be distrustful.

If a child is hated, he could become schizophrenic. What God expects from us is love. He can not love his neighbor if he doesn't love himself. Then he can love others and God. What you are is God's gift. What you become is your gift to God.

To change oneself is a slow process. Recognize and accept who you are. Love your neighbor especially the positive. Accept others as they are with their good. Love helps others become better, not our realization of our ideals.

Love is kind and patient. Love is understanding and enduring in all things. (The Living Bible, The Way 1 Corinthians 13:4)

Affirmations

My communication is clear. I accept my good. I let go of all expectation. I am loved and I am safe. I have the right to be me. I forgive the past. I know who I am. I touch others with love. I now discover how wonderful I am. I choose to love and enjoy myself. I love and accept myself at every age. Each moment in my life is perfect. I easily and comfortably release that which I no longer need in my life. I lovingly forgive myself. I am free. It is safe now for me to take charge of my own life. I choose to be free. I love and approve of myself. Life supports me and loves me. God takes care of my life. I trust life. I declare peace and harmony within me and around me. All is well. I deserve to feel good. I choose to create life that is joyous and abundant. I am at ease. Life is eternal and filled with joy.

I look forward to every moment. I am free to circulate love and joy in every part of my world. I love life. I only create peaceful experiences because I love myself.

3-21-85 For Past Lives

Sometimes you will feel you are making it up. But you will write it down and think about it. Close your eyes and see your bathroom. Look for the colors. What is on the wall? See all the objects.

Some will be stronger than others. Like now close your eyes and see yourself in childhood. It comes like a fantasy movie, right? This comes from your own subconscious mind which can't tell the difference between imagination and reality. If you feel you can see, play, and make it up. It will be like a dream so write it out.

General Past Life Regression

Have you lived before? If so, where? What time? Who were you? Man or woman? You can gain a better understanding of your present life.

From experiences that we plant in our past lives from harvest, to hardships, to physical or mental problems, it is possible to reconstruct your present life by releasing yourself of all the negativity of the past.

Karma

Balancing karma—this is the most easy to understand, the mechanical kind of cause and effect. A man who is born blind because as a soldier he purposely blinded another. A woman can not have a child because she abandoned her child in a past life. Balancing karma depends upon the situation as to how fast and effective the results will be.

Physical Karma—The misuse of the body in one life results in an appropriate affliction in a later life. A woman is born with lung problems that came from excess smoking and death from lung cancer in a past life.

Why do you choose your parents? Why do you come to earth? A man is born with a large birthmark on his leg carried over from a terrible burn.

False Fear Karma—a traumatic past life incident generates a fear that is not valid in the context of the current life. A woman is overweight in this life. In a past life, she was pretty, and others executed her. She believes if you want to be safe you have to be ugly. She cries out in regression.

False Guilt Karma—A person takes on the responsibility or accepts blame for a past life incident for which is a blameless driver of car accidentally crippled a child. It was not his fault and blames himself. He seeks self- forgiveness.

Developed Ability/ Awareness of Karma

Awareness is developed over a period of many lifetimes.

A man in Rome became interested in music and began to develop his ability. Today after six lifetimes is a professional musician. A woman married for thirty- five years refines her awareness of a human relationship. You came to learn again because you did not learn before.

If you don't have problems to challenge you, there could be no growth. In many problems, situations will not change but your viewpoint will change. A master accepts others as they are without attempting to change them to be what he wants them to be. You can not blame but accept karma because you set it up to experience opportunities so as to become aware of your true self within.

How much do you let yourself know of your own truth?

Viewpoints on everything from sex, career, money, relationships, and more are mastered by some people. Some feel insecure about money. Jane doesn't want to love her money because in another lifetime she had to take care of a child of a sick wealthy woman who had a nervous breakdown. In this lifetime she has fear of money.

Frank could not trust his wife because in a past life his wife had been in love with another man and left him.

If you are negative, you are full of fear. Do what you want to be or change your life to get where you want to go.

Karma is a Hindu word that means action. Karma is not punishment in the sense that we punish evildoers but rather a balancing out of energies. Like Math you know 2 plus 2 is four. Why not five?

Could one of you tell me God said the law to live was to love one another as ourselves not more or less? God did not want us to be unhappy. He just told us to love God and men as ourselves.

Just like the red light if you pass it, you might get hurt. So, we pay just like we pay with money. We pay sooner or later. If you feel a lot of anger with a person, the person might get irritations and go away or fight you. It's like a magnet drawing two persons into a fight or love. There is a saying "the devil made me do it" that time.

Why is a person an alcoholic? You came to learn what you can do in this lifetime because you did not learn. Or you hurt someone as they the alcoholic is doing now. You can choose your karma or change.

So, you can't control others. You can tell them how you feel but let them do for themselves. You can't change someone who does not want to change. If you were born poor, you might want to be rich or feel it is a sin.

All I can say is do the best you can and go within. Do a picture of how you would like your life to be. Next write out the money you would like to get and burn it.

Past life affects your present life with your talents, abilities, negative health problems, troubles, relationship conflict, fears, phobias, and wisdom.

Ask anything you would like to ask to open group. The church says the soul is spiritual. Theology says we are made of atomic physical matter.

May 1, 1985, Intensifying Déjà vu Potential happens whenever you touch on the subject or timing of one of your past lives. This could be while reading a book, watching TV, movie, or visiting a new environment. If you experienced a past life that relates, you'll sense an internal alarm that will make you aware.

One of the most important parts is to use this information for change in your life. Yes, you can change yourself, after all you did it to yourself. The way you think is who you are. Don't try to change people. Write down everything negative and see how much negative you have. Change it to the past. Don't send negative. Send love.

Pray to do a wish. Ask about the group; ask to say something nice about the other person.

July 14, 1985, Things to do. Health for the person.

What do you eat?
Watch what you do think when you are eating?
What do you drink? Water is the best drink.
Exercise. Walk, do Yoga, or do (Brain Gym).
What do you breathe and how do you breathe?
Meditation.
Study. When you stop learning you die.
Play and have fun. People don't stop playing because they are old. They stop playing and get old.
Goals. Never have just one goal.
To heal yourself, you have to think positive, not negative.
Feel the Spirit. Bring the Spirit in yourself.
I am in the hand of the Spirit. Put it with an aura. 1:30 p.m. July 14, 1985, with Dr. Roberts

Sylvia Sáenz M.Ed.

You have to smell the roses and count your blessings

Enjoy life. Work at it. Laughter is good for the soul and the body. Walking is also good. It is good for the heels of your feet. Meditation is also good. If someone in the family is ill, is it the person or the whole family who is ill? Why do you act like you do? A girl who was in trouble with all kinds of sickness, asked the doctor "Why am I sick?" Sometimes being sick helps some to get more care.

There is one great self, the divine being. There is always a reason for being sick. There are three causes of sickness: getting hurt, down cycle, and how you think. You get better the same way.

There are ups and downs in life. 1) How to do, 2) smile, and 3) think good thoughts. Make a list of ups and downs on your feelings.

Ask yourself when I think about my sickness, do I push to be sick or getting well. People don't stop playing because they grow old, they grow old because they stop playing.

There is a channel which passes messages to the front of the brain. Put white light in front of the head then let it in the channel then go around again. Do back front, then back then back to front for one day.

Sickness was sent from God, was the belief of people from long ago, and that only sickness could be taken by God.

First dream will tell you about the sickness. Next dream will tell you how to get well.

When others talk about a name there is power in the name of a person or through a photo.

Meeting Dr. Roberts July 14, 1985

If you want to feel better from a sickness:
Close left nostril, breathe with right nostril. Close right nostril breathe with left nostril.

Or do it with water and drink it. Heat water for sickness. Visualize a waterfall and see yourself getting well.

To be able to talk 3-23-1986

½ teaspoon salt
½ teaspoon baking soda
¾ cup warm bath
Every hour first day
Then four times a day

Applied Psycho-energy Mental Development Life Cycles

One to Seven Years—relate to outside world

Seven to Fourteen Years—physical development, sexual changes

Fourteen to Twenty-One Years—balance in physical, mental, and psychic awareness

Sylvia Sáenz M.Ed.

Twenty-One to Twenty-Eight Years—Emotional Development

Twenty-Eight to Thirty-Five Years—major mental development. Business and inventions thrive. Harmonize with Conscious Consciousness.

35 years to 42 years—Restlessness, Development, and Investigation in mysterious occult subjects.

42 years to 49 years—Discovery of meditation, spiritual development, and mystic tendencies.

49 years to 56 years—Tendency to separate from ego toward spiritual development.

56 years to 63 years—Full spiritual development.

What do you want from another person?

You don't own me. You're not mine and I'm not yours. Don't give orders.

A woman is made of glass, but you shouldn't try to break her because you shouldn't break what you can't mend. Put yourself in another person's shoes.

Cause and Effect of Mind

1) Influence. Send light to person who is trying to put you down.
2) You are the ruler of your life.
3) Ambience. Where do you live? Who are your friends?
4) You can change yourself. You cannot change people.

5) Give love to the people who don't like you. Ask for forgiveness and you cut the cord. Our parents give us programs, but we can change it.
6) Astral body survives death. 44

Chakras

Spirit (purple)

Thought (indigo)

Ether (turquoise)

Aire (green)

Fire (yellow)

Water (orange)

Earth (red)

Albahaca Florida Water—Ruda Albahaca flower is used to cleanse your home. 45

Saint Germain—Remember

Your mistakes are not important. What is important is the experienced you have gained from your errors.

Human Aura is about 12 inches around the individual and grows with development and human potential of his/her thoughts.

To transfer energy:

1) Close your eyes.
2) Breathe deeply.
3) Activate your imagination.
4) Treatment—minimal time is three minutes.

The one applying energy requires complete health. Remember a sentence said with devotion elevates the vibration tone of the person who receives and gives.

Divisions of the Mind

Objective Mind

1	2	3
Instincts	Individual Values Programs	Ego

Ways to Change

See what you should change.

Write all the positives.

Read two times a day what you wrote.

Work with levels—visualize the situation realized.

Reflect on the necessity of the change you want to see.

For 30 days saying I am going to _____ and feel great about it.

The Secret

Imagination, Emotion, Love, Burning Desire, and Enthusiasm

If you use love, you have everything. If you love yourself, you can love others, but you have to learn to forgive.

Level of Mind

Profound Alpha

Sleeping Receptor

Love Magnetic Mold

No Manipulation

Use your imagination to prevent deep sleep. Today at night I will forgive _____.

(The Book of Gold of St.Gemain)

Imagination

Secret

Burning Desire   Emotion
(Enthusiasm)   (Love)

51

Plant experiment proves all thought managed with determination has the power to be realized. The experiment should last minimum of 30 days with 10 minutes daily of concentration applying magnetic mold.

The first thing that captivates subconscious is the intention of another.

Telepathic thought should only be used for reconciliation, for the ill, to bring benefit to another.

Cerebral Pulses

35—Danger Zone

30—Risk Zone

23—Beta

15—Alpha

7—Theta

1—Delta

The best treatment of fever is alternating hot and cold applications. Any cold applications over 15-20 minutes can cause internal congestion. The greater the mass of water applied the greater the effect. In all recorded history various baths were used in the treatment of diseases. 49

Do not apply heat to the feet of a diabetic. Only apply heat to the stomach of a diabetic. Hydrotherapy can not have a toxic effect. It is not a science. Some unfavorable reactions to hydrotherapy are headaches, dizziness, shivering, and nausea. Some benefits of cold packs are relief of pain, and reduction of inflammation. The effect of alternate hot and cold is reduction of pain locally and distally alternate contraction and dilation of blood vessels.

Other types of hydrotherapy procedures are salt glows, douches, and enemas. Three forms of hydrotherapy include water, steam, and ice. Three types of fever are adaptive, artificial, or hormonal.

Marta De Leon— Muscles

Trapezius muscle, some functions with the Vagus Nerve accessory nerves.

Vison, optic nerves, sense of smell olfactory nerves.

The skull does not move but with a hit it moves.

If a person walks in and says he has a problem with a disc you can work with them with massage because if they had a problem with a disc they would not walk.

More pain is found in the T2, 7 or 8T. The lungs are there. The flow of blood does not go to the head.

Thirty percent of one's weight is muscle.

Movement and relaxing are good for the muscle.

Muscles are not good with a lot of fat.

Muscles work with hormones facia tissue in the skin.

Smokers do not have oxygen.

Muscles come in smaller, fat, thin and long.

Muscles overworked shake nervously:

1) Motor movement
2) Sensory feeling

Cerebellum controls balance when balance is lost you think or feel too much or too little.

08/02/1990 Massage helps the liver before running. It helps the lactic acid not to overwork, because lactic acid is what causes hurt. If you do too much work, you get lactic acid and it's hard for you to do the work. If you do not eat right your muscles get fatigued. Fat is energy and it is for doing more work. Lactic acid turns blue.

Myelin sheath allows electrical impulses to transmit quickly and efficiently along the nerve cells to help movement.

With stimulation motor neurons release neurotransmitters from axon terminals.

You need oxygen because without it you can't think the same.

When you take a deep breath, you think better.

It is good for the baby to crawl because the right and left brain will work better. If the baby can not it may have some learning disabilities.

+ gives you strength

-will make you weak

Work with + in your head.

Use X pattern with left and right hands and legs.

There are people who say they want to change but they don't want to.

Take a sea salt bath after taking treatment for cancer.

If you are eating, you have to chew and chew for the saliva to work in your stomach.

Sympathetic nervous system—responds with fight or flight.

Parasympathetic nervous system responds by freezing.

Neurons send messages to all parts of the body to and from sensory or motor.

Microglia clears away debris, and fights infections.

Cell processes or nerve fibers have different diameters and no dendrites to the cell body.

Axon is away from the cell body. Myelin is a white protein substance that surrounds many but not all nerve fibers help to protect and regenerate.

Efferent neurons send signals from the brain to muscles, glands, and organs of the body in response to sensory input.

For skin protection water comes out for temperature regulation.

Never give a person something to complain about because they will.

After 40 years old the skin begins to age. The older the person is the thinner the skin will become.

At the age of 23 years old your bones are full.

If the hip is broken, the foot will be out all the way.

The power is two brains. The order is in the back of the brain. The front of the brain shows us what to do. Learn to say no when you don't want to do something and when you know what is right and wrong.

One pair of muscles and one does the work. Muscles are different. When you touch a person, you are telling the person to change what hurts. Start with your feet; that will tell you what to change. They answer the tune, and the mind can answer.

Maria Gloria Delua Sáenz (my mother)'s words:

At almost 50 years old and still achieving. After automobile accident that brought suffering and pain with a TMJ diagnosis, she became inspired to pursue a career as a message therapist in order to help people to relieve physical and mental fatigue.

"I thank God first, then my doctors, who helped me back to health, Dr. Ramos, Dr. Goldsmith, and Dr. Yee, as well as my therapists, Hunts, Donna, and Lucy. My mother said: "also I give thanks to my teacher Noemi Norton, Judy Ibarra, and Mary Riley, who helped me in the massage therapy studies. In addition, I would like to express my thanks to all those involved in the Love and Happiness through Motivation organization (my mother's group.)"

"Although health wise I had regressed, my career took a different shape. I felt deeply inspired after receiving numerous calls from Love and Happiness through Motivation Organization whose members needed me to continue teaching and helping others. And my massage therapy courses prove to be one step further in helping others."

"Thanks to all who have given me encouragement," shares Maria Gloria Delua Sáenz.

Maria Gloria Delua Sáenz, as you know her, as a counselor with a DTH (Doctor of Theology), now is a registered massage therapist with a Texas License of 3900.

Now back to my mom's massage training

Cryotherapy with cold applications or ice have been used extensively in Sports Medicine. It decreases pain, muscle spasm, metabolism, and increases circulation. For heat if used too soon it will increase secondary hypoxic injury and swelling.

Ice, compression, and elevation are used almost universally for immediate care of sports injuries; to control swelling and decrease the magnitude of the hematoma.

Initially the ice bag should be applied for 30 minutes then removed. After one hour and 30 minutes reapplied for an additional 30 minutes to continue throughout the evening.

All exercise should be performed pain-free and progress as fast as possible.

Cryostretch for relief of muscle spasm. Exercises consist of a combination of static stretching (passive) and contact relax technique of proprioceptive neuromuscular facilitation (active).

Effects of Heat

Rate and volume of blood flow increases. Metabolism in tissue increases. Muscles relax.

Analgesic (relieves pain). Increases circulation. Vasodilation (decreases blood pressure.)

Effects of Cold

Circulation is slowed down. Metabolism is slowed down. Analgesic (for sprains, and burns.)

Effects of Paraffin Bath

1. Hyperemia and other effects of local heat.
2. Preparation of the skin for massage by making it smooth, soft, and pliable.

Contrast Bath

The immersion of a body part alternately in hot and cold waters.

Effects of Contrast Baths

1. Alternate contraction and dilation of blood vessels (vascular exercise).
2. Marked increase of blood flow locally and reflexively. Derivative effect.
3. Increased local metabolism hastens healing.

Complete Alcohol Rub- great with bed ridden fevers. It's the application of rubbing alcohol to the surface of the body.

Effects and Indications of Complete Alcohol Rub

1. For a cooling effect after general or local application of heat.
2. To lower body temperature in fevers.
3. To protect pressure areas by the astringent effect on the skin.
4. To refresh the patient when a bath is not given.

Diabetics—never apply heat to the feet.

Reflexology Paige Aster Jan. 15-16, 1983

Diseases by Organs Glands

Adrenals

Controls muscles tone in body

Anger

Arthritis

Asthma

Low Blood Pressure

Constipation

Emotions

Emphysema

Fluid, Retention

Insomnia

Ovaries

Overweight

Shock

Stress

Archilles Tendon

Cysts, Ovaries

Hemorrhoids

Kidney infections

Sciatic

Sexual problems

Diaphragm

Breathing problems

Angina Pectoris

Heart

Anemic

Ileocecal Valve

Asthma

Bronchial Problems

Constipation

Dandruff

Emphysema

Eczema

Hemorrhoids

Lungs

Migraines

Sinus

Kidney

Eczema

Gout

Liver

Anemic

Anger

Edema

Migraines

Lower Back

Lower Backache

Constipation

Lymphatics

Constipation

Edema

Eczema

Parathyroid

Arthritis

Bones (Calcium)

Cramps, Legs

Pituitary

Arthritis

Edema

Emotions

Urinary

Sigmoid Flexure

Constipation

Gas

Sinuses

Asthma

Breast Problems

Dandruff

Migraines

Solar Plexus

Anemic

Anger

Arthritis

Asthma

High Blood Pressure

Breathing Problems

Chest

Emotions

Relax

Tension

Spine

Anemic (corpuscles built in bones)

Anger (feeds energy for the anger)

Spleen

Anemic

Thyroid

High Blood Cholesterol, Emotions

Tonsils

Health in Your Hands Eastern Diagnosis Techniques July 1983 John Mann

"If your grip is weak your heart is not as strong as it should be. Hand crushing grip probably high blood pressure and an overactive heart."

"If your hands are whitish pale shade, or if you constantly have them plunged into your pockets, you are likely a shallow breather, with congested and under-active lungs. Taking a daily long brisk walk with deep breathing and a full swing of your arms, is a terrific way to activate and stabilize the functions of the respiration and circulation."

Index finger that bends inward toward thumb often appears in a person whose colon is overly contracted and hardened from overconsumption of eggs, meat, and salt.

A stiff or rigid thumb often shows an accumulation of fats in the corresponding lung.

"The thumb is traditionally considered to represent the faculties of logic, reason, will, and the thinking "I" in general. The influence of the lung meridian along the thumb is clearly a key factor in this correlation, as the brain is the body's major user of oxygen."

"The small intestine is the point in the body where our external, environment (in the form of good) finally comes into direct contact with our bloodstream or internal environment through absorption. Not surprisingly, the side of hand below the little finger, hosting the small intestine meridian, is considered in palmistry to represent the faculties of intuition, instinct, and an intimate awareness of the environment and nature's rhythms. The radial side of the hand, and the little finger, the ulnar side, relate physiologically to the uppermost organs (lungs and brain) and lowermost area (small intestine) respectively. They are referred to as showing conscious thought and subconscious or gut knowledge.

Thumb—lung meridian regulates respiration, renewal of blood, vitality of cells

First finger—large intestine meridian regulates water in the body and elimination.

Second finger—heart meridian (governor)—regulates overall energy, circulation, reproductive functions, blood, and lymph.

Third finger—triple heater meridian regulates overall metabolism, body heat and temperature control.

Little finger—heart meridian—regulates heart and cardiovascular functions—small intestine—regulates absorption.

"If hands are hot or reddish—too much eating, drinking, particularly sweets, oil alcohol, sugar or fruit; heart and metabolism in general are overworking and temperament may be overactive, volatile, or impulsive."

"If hands are cold and wet, your heart is weakened by a long-term consumption of too much fruit, sugar, or excessive liquids; if cold and dry, the capillaries are contracted, possibly from consuming too much salt, animal food, or overcooked foods. Wet palms generally show more than fluids in the body, with corresponding overworked bladder, kidneys, and lungs."

"Check the area just below your wrist on the back of the arm. If this area is puffy, swollen, or thick, this shows a long-time accumulation of fats and mucus in the upper body, often creating a predisposition towards cancer in the lung, throat or thyroid (the corresponding diagnostic area for lower body would be the area around the Achilles tendon.)"

"Specific hand gestures can often reveal particular blockages. Constant tapping or strumming the fingers, usually shows an excessive intake of fruits, sugar, or other expansive substances, together with an overactive imagination and excessive conscious thinking. Nervous tapping of the feet usually shows more intake of eggs, meat, salt, and other more heavy, constrictive foods, with over acute senses and an inability to think openly.

Stiff or awkward hand gesture usually reveal some degree of insincerity or less than wholehearted convictions. Arms folded stoically over the chest often express a stagnation and underactivity of the lungs; hands held shyly down and behind the back often accompany deposits of fat around the kidneys, and reproductive organs. Hands held in the front pockets are often serving to protect a weakness in the large intestine and lungs; in the back pockets, small intestine, and heart; and on the hips, large intestine, kidneys, and the bladder."

"The characteristic elbow on the table, sometimes with the head on the chin resting on the fist or hand of that arm, shows

Sylvia Sáenz M.Ed.

that the colon on that side of the body is sluggish and lacks power."

"Of course, any all these gestures may be assumed for expressive purposes without necessarily indicating health problems, and a person who enjoys good health naturally assumes dozens of hand postures and gestures. But it is the person who chronically uses one or two specific patterns, someone who would not be comfortable unless assuming that posture, who is unconsciously trying to reinforce or balance a weakened or stagnated energy in the body."

"On the other hand, many features are used not to balance ill health but to positively direct our energy in a certain way. The classic prayer posture, meditation postures, and all such uniting of the hands, are used as a means to bring our energies into a restful state of balance, often to achieve a higher state of judgment or perspective. The simple act of waving is also a way of showing our inner feelings."

Pathology and Reflex Points -January 15-16, 1983-Reflexology Seminar Paige Asten

Constipation —clogging up of the entire system
     —should have a good stool after very meal
     —have constipation if tongue is coated
     —for every disease try to help person eliminate
     —work colon, small intestine, sigmoid flexure, ileocecal valve, lymphatics, liver, lower back, adrenals (controls muscle tone in body)

Cramps, legwork parathyroids

Cysts, ovaries—work ovaries, and up sides or Archilles tendon 4 to 6 inches

Dandruff—is mucus—ileocecal valve and sinuses

Diabetes
    —diabetes mellitus absence of insulin
    —always thirsty
    —muscle wasting
    —stimulate pancreas, other glands

Edema
    —extra accumulation of salt
    —swollen ankles
    —causes—poisons, toxins
    —most common cause—congested kidneys
    —stimulate all lymph points, kidneys, bladder, liver, pituitary

Emotions
    —first place to feel emotion is in the stomach—work solar plexus
    —if you don't cry enough, work bladder
    —worries, lot on mind—work big toe (brain)
    —calming emotional upset—work solar plexus, thyroid, big toe, adrenals, kidneys, pituitary

Emphysema—work lungs, bronchial, ileocecal valve, adrenals

Eczema—colon, ileocecal valve, lymphatics—most important kidneys

Fluids, retention—work adrenals

Gout—work kidneys

Gallbladder, work gallbladder inside 4th toe (next to pinkie)

Gas—sigmoid flexure (under the bladder)

Hemorrhoids—work ileocecal valve (muscle that separates small and large intestine above the appendix), heel up the back leg, coccyx (small triangle bone at the base of the spinal column)

Hip—work around the outside of the ankle, triangle

Inner ear—behind the 4th toe

Insomnia—adrenals

Kidney Infections—kidney, ureters (tubes made of smooth muscle that propel urine from kidneys to the urinary bladder), bladder, up sides of Achilles tendon

Lungs—ileocecal valve

Lymphatics—on the top of the foot, at base of the 4th toe, powerful drain work gently—from over the top of foot to ankle bone.

Menopause—work uterus

Migraine—a migraine is only a symptom of the real problem caused by any of the organs of the body—stomach, intestines, ileocecal valve, sinuses, or liver.

Ovaries—adrenals

Overweight adrenals

Pregnancy—do not stimulate uterus—may cause abortion or early delivery

Relax—solar plexus, big toe work and shake

Sciatic—sciatic nerve ends in web between big and 1st toe—4th lumbar vertebrae, sciatic band bottom of foot (heel), under ankles, Achilles tendon, triangle

Sexual problems—work up sides of Achilles tendon 4-6 inches

Shock   —heart rate up, muscles, have goose bumps, not smooth, constipated
                —fear, fright, flight
                —work heart, adrenals

Sinus—ileocecal valve connected to sinuses, produces mucus membrane in the intestines which is transported up to the head and chest sinuses

Smoking—work grooves on the top of the foot

Sore throat   —determine degree of sore throat on the top at the base of the big toe.
                —if sore, work around top and outside of big toe.

Stress—adrenals

Tension—solar plexus, big toe, and shake

Thrombosis —blood clot in blood vessels
—from sport injuries, sclerosis (sideways, curvature of the spine)

Thyroid —hyperthyroid—too much thyroxin
—symptoms—pop eyes, thin, craving sugars, food, never still, can only sleep 2-3 hours at a time, always hot, high rates of everything, nervous, apprehensive

Underactive —symptoms
thyroid

—less energy and heat produced
—don't want to get up at all
—sleep a lot
—gain weight easily
—always cold

Tonsils—around big toe, thyroid, between big and first toe

Urinary—work pituitary

Fore Brain	Back Brain
Adult	Parent
Now	Past Experiences
Awareness	Vertical Auricular line

Dominant/Alternate Brain Function

Right	Left
Creative	Analytical

Spiritual	Linear
Focused on Whole	Specific Focus
Unlimited Perception	Survival
No Time Limitation	Time-oriented
	Verbal language 71
Language; Image/Color/Symbols	Self-image
Rhythmic/Musical	Judgmental
Non-judgmental	Belief system
No fear	

Basic Massage Contraindications

Diabetes-Definition—any of several metabolic disorders, excessive urine discharge. Find out when and where had last insulin shot—especially light message of that area—don't want to spread the insulin to fast in the body, no deep strenuous massage, can put too much strain on the arteries and veins. Gentle, light massage, special attention to pancreas and digestive areas.

Phlebitis: Inflammation of the veins, usually in the arms and legs. No deep massage—need to avoid hemorrhaging. Move blood back to heart.

Low blood pressure: careful of relaxing, sedating the heart and body systems too much. Stimulating massage.

Disease is congestion—a clogged system, need to work to:

1) Get rid of wastes
2) Improve circulation in blood and lymph
3) Stimulate systems and organs to function

Remember—you want to strengthen the body and increase vitality and stimulate body functions, not weaken the body nor take away energy that is needed for healing!

Reflections

1) God loves me.
2) I have to love myself first.
3) I have to say what they want me to say.
4) I am important as I let myself be.
5) Who am I?
6) Who do I want to be?
7) I choose where I want to be?
8) I am learning it is okay to make mistakes.
9) I don't stop habits until I want to stop them.
10) God sends me people to make me happy.
11) Life is a game. We play the way we want.

Ask yourself what do I have to learn?

Reflections (cont.)

What self-talk or what others say is not true?
Don't make others fight your battles.
Face your fears.
What do I judge like my parents did?

Meditation

First get in a chair, sit, and breathe in and out deeply. Go to the top of a hill and leave all the problems behind you. You feel more sure of yourself than you have feel in your life. How does it feel to have no worries?

What would happen if you went higher? And how do you feel when you come back down from the hill?

My mother achieved so much in her life. Her main intent was "did I help as many people as I could have?"

She was in Lowell Elementary School in the 1960's.

Even though she studied up to 7th grade, interrupted to earn money due to poverty, she went on to finish her GED and later obtained her Doctorate Degree in Metaphysics, but she always remained humble. She attended Pan American University in Edinburg, Texas. She worked hard to make herself and others happy. She believed she could do anything because "with God all things are possible," one of her favorite sayings. With a cup full of kindness giving to others, the world loved her. She had an uncanny ability to listen and understand others, while others, even the shyest person, would pour out their life stories. People came from everywhere to take her classes. She was written up in the newspaper.

She had to learn about self-respect from feeling she couldn't to learning she could. Self-respect came when she learned to love herself and say "I love you" in the mirror.

She said, "the sun comes out for me and everyone else in the same way."

Rest is part of self-respect. Realize no one is like you. Taking care of oneself is self-love. Also not being co-dependent by needing others more than they need you.

Say "I am important to me." "To look and to feel are different." You may look one way but feel different.

What would you do if you were honest about your wants and needs?

Would you put yourself first? Would you talk with people who put you up? Would you pray more?

What is self-acceptance?

Feeling you are enough.
Feeling you are wanted and loved.
Taking care of oneself.
Saying and doing our best with the tools we have.
Feeling abundant and worthy.
Helping oneself to help others.
Feeling you can be who you really are.
Feeling happy in who you are.
Love oneself.
Be best self.
Understanding oneself.
To feel important and free.
Finding oneself.

Self-Acceptance

If you are only good when you are pleasing others, then others don't deserve you. Forgive others. Be with people who make you feel wanted, needed, who really listen, and understand. Look for happiness. Receive and give and love. Allow yourself to be cared for and allow yourself to care for others. Be honest.

See yourself and others as they are. Believe in yourself. Don't allow yourself to be controlled. Be yourself. Love yourself. Have fun and be free.

My mom was a healer, and empathetic. She used journaling as a coping skill. As a conversationalist, she shared her ideas with other people and listened to their ideas. She realized having problems does not mean we are defective or inferior. She also would make time for reflection and would study metaphysical subjects and all kinds of religions and cultures. She loved history. She definitely made time to make herself pretty. Mom would often say: "with God all things are possible."

My mom's favorite songs include:

One Day at a Time
Downtown
Que Será, Que Será (What will be, will be)
These Boots are Made for Walking
I Am Woman
Ain't That Just the Way
Shoo Fly Don't Bother Me
His Got the Whole World in His Hands
Johnny Cash's songs
Isidro Lopez's songs
Augustin Lara's songs
My song "Lord, This Christmas"

Her songs:

I am Whole.
Free, Free, Free

I am Whole

I am whole. I am free. I have that special light in me.
Jesus sends from above giving me peace and love.
I am perfect. I am perfect. I am free.

Free, Free, Free

Free, Free, Free
I wanna be free, free, free
Like the birds up in the tree, tree, tree.
Just together you and me, me, me.

My mother's advice:

You can not do much how others behave, but you can do
something about how you feel.

Learn from your mistakes.

Mom's favorite sayings:

The light of God will be with me.

Yo conocí el amor, en mi fue tracionero (I knew love for me
I was betrayed).

Don't believe everything you hear and believe only half of
what you see.

9/4/1989

Find the positive.
Say:
Mind, create positive conditions for my goals to come to be.
Mind, reject this physical manifestation. Return all organ systems to normal function.
Mind, reject and go to the opposite.
My mind is fine and follows a positive situation.
Mind, release unnecessary tension from my body.
Mind, create positive condition for (you say it).
Mind, return all systems to normal function.

Find something that you like (in your mind or literally).
Make a hand to push buttons to release stress (in your mind or literally).

Say: "Mind, release all unnecessary tension from the muscles in my head, chest, back, small intestines, large intestines, legs, feet, and hands.
More and more tension release. More and more relaxation come in."

Enjoy all the relaxation. Feeling good now.

In my mom's words: "In 1959 I was married to Zeferino Sáenz. I moved from Elsa, Texas where I had lived all my life to Chicago, Illinois. My goal was to return to Texas with something new and different in 1970.

I returned to McAllen, Texas but with three little ones. In Chicago I had to work on helping people with jobs as a teacher aide and a nurse aide.

I enjoyed being around people and meeting people. My thought was "what can I bring to the valley which is new and different."

Then in 1978, a phone call came in where I was invited to Waco, Texas to receive training. I thought "in what way can I help people?" The thought came "why not help people help themselves?"

After her training, people came from everywhere to take my mom's classes and she came out in the newspaper.

The tape presentation included world leading psychiatrists. Its purpose was to help people understand oneself, make personality behavior change, as well as enjoy life and improved relationships with one another.

Paul J. Meyer outlines for use his Million Dollar Personal Plan

Who am I?
What activities in your life give you the greatest sense of accomplishment?

For my mom, a few activities that brought her joy were:

1) Reading a good book
2) Dancing
3) Nice house
4) Decorating
5) Helping people
6) Having family and friends over

What activities give you the least sense of accomplishment?

For my mom, a few activities:

1) Not being on time
2) Worrying
3) Having to ask
4) Criticizing

What are your goals?

A few for my mother were:

1) Having a house
2) Getting a GED
3) To be a good mother
4) Having good health
5) Having faith in God, the future and herself

Please describe your goals as specifically as possible.

Before writing on this page, take a minute or two to review what you have written. Then list below the things that you feel are your most important sources of motivation. Explain why they motivate you.

I think about who encourages you, and who discourages you.

Think about who allows you to take risks, and who cautions you.

My mom knew how to give love from her heart. In her words: "I knew how to give from the heart." "I live tomorrow and many days more and God will bless me. Something I must never forget is that God is love and I have a lot of him because I have love."

Her goal was to be a psychologist. What she did become was a metaphysical teacher/life coach with a Doctorate Degree in Metaphysics.

Her values included family, self-improvement, acquiring useful knowledge, sleep, work, relaxation, play, and not to waste time. She acknowledged finishing your education before marriage should be a priority and instilled it in her children. She believed in having a plan of action to be successful.

According to her, the greatest accomplishments were the jobs she obtained and her family. Her jobs included factory worker, teacher aide, nurse aide, and saleslady before she became self-employed as a Metaphysical/Spiritual teacher.

Part of her many trainings included Success Motivation Institute, and Joy Course by Global Relationship Center, Inc. She learned self-acceptance; it's ok to make a mistake; and intention in being more in control of the results you want to get with your goals.

My mother's determination kept her from giving up on improving herself. Others criticized her speech (annunciation) of words since she only went to Jr. High School and was taught in English when she spoke in Spanish. That didn't stop her from being successful. She went on to get her G.E.D., attended college, and later obtained her Doctorate Degree in Metaphysics.

She would criticize others with the intention to help improve them. Part of her development included psychodrama group therapy.

My mother began her Success Motivation Institute Training on 9/5/78. She felt encouraged by her friendships and her children. She considered Dr. Augustin Ramirez, a psychologist in Chicago, Illinois to be the most successful person she had ever met. He also was a Catholic priest and mentored her. He spoke seven languages and wrote several psychology books including one on psychodrama.

My mother admired Dr. Augustin Ramirez because his work was play, a way of life. He had everything he ever wanted and could find good even in sick people.

Some of the books my mother read were: "I'm Ok, You're Ok," "Successful Real Estate Selling Memory Magic," "The Art of Public Speaking," "The Richest Man in Babylon," "How to Overcome Discouragement," "Your Child's Self Esteem," "The Key to Motivation," "Think and Grow Rich," "Psycho-Cybernetics," "How to be a Success in Life Insurance," and "Tough Minded Management."

Sylvia Sáenz M.Ed.

Maria Delua Sáenz

McAllen, Texas
Maria Delua Sáenz would like to reach the souls of people to
discover their higher potential.

EDUCATION

Ph.D.-Theology

EXPERIENCE

Nurse aide-5 years
Factory worker-(punch press) 1 year
Saleslady (various locations including Montgomery Ward)-20
years
Massage therapist-10 years
Teacher aide-2 years (Gang Prevention Coordinator)

SKILLS

Bilingual-English and Spanish speaking
Public Relations Specialist

ACCOMPLISHMENTS

Offered college scholarship
Mother of 3 children

Hobbies

Artist-painting (worked on art project for "After the Rain Comes Sun" CD which title of painting was "Splash Awakening")

Other artistic projects paintings include Mural of 7 Angels, "Miracle Guardian Angel", and "Spiritual Healing: Agape Indians of Hope, My Lupita, The Virgin Guadalupe"

Interior Decorating

Speaking and Listening

Affirmations

I approve of myself and the way I am changing.

I am doing the best I can

Each day gets easier.

I rejoice that I am in the rhythm and flow of my ever-changing life.

Today is a wonderful day. I choose to make it so.

All is well in my world.

I love myself.

I have a unique job.

I am all perfect, whole, and complete.

My unique creative talents, abilities flow through me and are expressed in deeply satisfying ways.

There are people out there who are always looking for my services.

I am always in demand, and I can pick and choose what I want to do.

I earn good money doing what satisfies me.

My work is a joy and a pleasure.

I love myself therefore I behave and think in a loving way to all people for I know that which I give out returns to me multiplied.

I only attract loving people in my world for they are a mirror of who I am.

I love myself therefore I forgive and totally release the past and past experiences.

I am free.

I love myself therefore I live totally in the now experiencing each moment as good knowing that my future is bright, joyous, and secure for I am a beloved child of the Universe, and the Universe takes care of me, now and forever more.

I live in harmony and balance.

As I internally create a pattern of self-worth, I no longer have the need to delay my good.

I am beginning to understand that I created this.

I now take my power back.

I am going to release the old ideas.

In the infinity of life where I am all is perfect, whole, and complete.

I live in harmony and balance with everyone.

I know deep at the center of my being there is an infinite well of love.

I now allow this love to flow to the surface. It fills my heart, my body, my mind, my consciousness, and my very being radiating out from me in all directions to returned and be multiplied.

The more love I use and give the more I have to give. The supply is endless.

The use of love makes me feel good. It is an expression of inner joy.

I love myself therefore I take loving care of my body. I love feeding it nourishing food.

Sylvia Sáenz M.Ed.

I lovingly groom my body and dress it and my lovingly body responds to me with vibrant health and energy.

I love myself therefore I provide for myself a comfortable home, one that fills all my needs and is a pleasure to be in.

I fill the room with the vibration of love so that all who enter myself included will feel loved and nourished.

I reinforce that which I learn in joyous ways.

My day begins with gratitude and joy.

I love who I am and all that I do.

I am a living, loving, joyous expression of life.

All is well in my world.

My mom's insights:

The light is a joy.

We are here to grow.

It is okay to do wrong. You're just one lifetime.

Hell is a state of mind.

Anger is a sin on yourself.

You can take it or learn from it.

Don't do things you have to do unless you feel like it.

When you pass on, your feelings are the same as on earth.

Don't be afraid to think because they made a mistake.

Take one step at a time to do anything.

You are as happy as you make your mind to be.

A poem mom would say.

"Como te miras me mire
Y como me miras te verás."
The way you are now, I once was.
The way I am now, one day you'll be.
Remember me as you pass by.
As I am now, one day you'll be.
Prepare for death and follow me.
Where I am now, one day you'll be.
Where you are now, I once was.

More Affirmations.

I open my heart and create only loving communication. I am safe. I am well. I am at peace with my own feelings. I am safe where I am. I create my own security.

More Insights,

If you don't believe you can do it, it's just wishful thinking.

Change the way you talk and change your life.

Sylvia Sáenz M.Ed.

Write: "I will remember my dream." Ask to dream to give you answers to what you need to know.

We must release resentment for others but first for ourselves.

More insights,

Be myself.

Be happy with what I know.

Do not get hurt easy.

Do your best to see what people are thinking.

More about my mom in her words:

"I like people."

"I like to hear how people think."

"I am not afraid to talk to people."

"I have good looks."

More about mom in her words,

"Dr. Father Augustine Ramirez was a very good friend. He asked me to help him help people. So, I went to help him in Chicago, Illinois. He cared for people and felt everyone was good and can get well with love. Did I learn from him or did God send me the feeling of care for people?"

"He would pray for the people. I came to the Valley to live, so we moved to Texas. I had three children and one husband who wanted to work for himself."

"I helped him then I wanted to do my own thing, but then I got pregnant and wanted the baby so much, but I lost the baby. I was so sad and went to church for help, but no one told me the answer I wanted to hear. Why did God take my baby?"

"It was the first time I didn't have to work; the first time I had a house of my own. I had three children, but I cried for the one I lost. They asked me to go to a grocery store in Mexico. This lady said when people change, the change goes to the other mother who can give him what he can learn because the world is like a school."

"I went to Mexico to learn. The lady said we pick our parents, and they teach us what we came to earth to do."

"So maybe my baby didn't want me after all. He wanted the other mother and that is why I lost my baby."